Born Of Ash

Diya Mehta

BookLeaf
Publishing

India | USA | UK

Made with ❤ on the BookLeaf Publishing Platform
www.bookleafpub.in
www.bookleafpub.com

Dedication

To those who have hated the system, the rules, the lies.
To the ones who have burned with rage at the world and
themselves.
This is for you—
Not to quiet the fire, but to set it free.

Preface

This book is not meant for everyone, it is meant for very few people and if you read this and relate to it - I understand your frustration.

There comes a moment when you look at the wreckage of everything you were taught to be—the torn pages, the burned bridges, the ruins of almosts—and realize that none of it defines you. You are not the fire that destroyed you. You are what rises from it.

This book is not just poetry. It is a reckoning. A reflection. A mirror held up to the self that existed before the world told you who to be.

I wrote this for the people who have ever felt trapped in a script they didn't write. Who has mistaken survival for freedom. Who has rebuilt the same cage over and over again, thinking it was a new beginning.
This is for the ones who have burned—and are still learning how to rise.

You are not broken. You are becoming

Acknowledgements

To my mentors who handed me matches when I needed to burn—thank you.

Especially To my parents who stood by the fire, unafraid —thank you.

To my brother, my sisters, and my friends who let me rebuild without telling me what it should look like— thank you.

To my past selves: I see you. You are not lost. You are a part of me still.

To those who read this book and recognise pieces of themselves in these pages—I hope you find in these words what you need. And if not, I hope they at least remind you that you are not alone in the fire.

And finally, to the words themselves—for being the only thing that ever truly understood me.

No one rises alone. Even the most solitary transformations are shaped by the echoes of those who have stood beside us, knowingly or not.

This book would not exist without all of you.

Neither would I.

STAGE 1

Torn Pages

The Preacher's Maze

What if I told you, that your dreams have all been
shattered
Shattered by not your beliefs, but your society
Not your society's shaming, but their preaching
Their lessons and their teachings

Everything this world is built on is a ruse
A psychological deal ordained for the goose
"Those that require support and guidance
Join us and you'll master your intelligence"

Its a circus all over
How crazy we're not rolling over
Laughing at the atrocity
That produces this grandiose waste

The core you stand on, is a shattering disgrace
For it killed your demons of shining grace
Demons that would have taken you farther
Than any circus-y maze

So lend me your hand
For I don't intend to preach you anything

Just to light a blaze within your soul once again
I desire to open your mind through this poetic frame.

3

Premature Pruning

The seedling sprouts in full bloom, outshining all others
The first ever of its kind, she glows through the darkest
of times

Novelty lead to fear, an automatic instantaneous
response
So others had to mold her, and erase the threat of her

They taught her the norms and constructs, rules she'd
now need to abide by
Made her a follower overnight, to dim her light

And for years on end she learnt and learnt, all that the
world had to offer
Silently forcing down the rules, only to destroy her own
bloom

Who knew learning could be so costly, costing her her
beaut
For had she not learnt the guide to growing up, she
could've devoured others' roots

Our schedules, so full—our souls, so hollow
Our resumes, so perfect—our hearts, so gallow

Our followers, so many—our true voice, so borrowed
Our life, so unique—yet our folklores run deep
This is the price of premature pruning.

The Conversation That Never Happened

Them: Sit up straight. Fix your hair. Speak clearly.
Me: I do. I did. I try.
Them: No, not like that. Like this.
Me: But this is how I am.
Them: Not enough. Never enough.
Me: But what is enough?
Them: A little more. Always a little more.
Me: When does it stop?
Them: When you become someone else.
Me: But then I won't be me.
Them: That's the point.

A Narrative Unfolds

I have no story to tell.
I will never believe that
I can make a difference.
I have always known that
I am powerless.
And no one can convince me that
Hope still lingers.
So rest assured, I will believe that
My narrative is set.
And I won't lie to myself that
My past does not define me.
But then—

(Tear here for a message for this poem)

(Look closer—there's more to Poem 5 than meets the
eye)

Unseen Threads

there are whispers we **D**o not hear,
Or maybe, we choose not to listen.
our feet step forward, **U**naware,
Behind us, echoes of the pas**T**.
Remember the s**I**lent hands,
Som**E**where in the dark, they **S**titch the pieces we forget.

(Is everything as it seems? Reread Poem 4 backwards.)

Unheard Dialogue

In this world that is ablaze
Our books are burning yearning,

Waiting to be consumed with all their fire;

But readers are busy untangling their lives
With instruments of partial knowledge,

Using means of incomplete teachings to guide their
power;

How did our social design change
From THE Homo Sapiens that could THINK

To being chimpanzees that do nothing but SINK SYNC.

Beware, for minds that cease to spark
Will fade to shadows in the dark.

Leaving behind souls tainted with dying marks.

Ghosts of Almost

A brushstroke—paused mid-air,
A sentence—cut short by hesitation,
A love—left waiting at the station,
A door—never fully closed,
A call—never made.
We live in the echoes of almosts,
In the spaces between what could have been,
The weight of words unspoken,
The ghosts of paths unwalked.
And in the end, we wonder—
Did we live?
Or did we just almost?

The tearing

Instructions: First read it independently, then tear along
the line to make a new poem.

|

|

The hours on the clock tick,
As I spend every minute questioning.
This stage feels wrong,
And I seem to be wavering.
My confidence at the shore,
So shallow, low, and gore.
The bleeding won't stop,
As my mind falls
into shattered pieces on the floor.
Your opinions are unwelcomed
At the revelation that threatened
This stage that I've built, is alas,
A mirage—
Collapsing fast, as I breathe my last.

|

|

The transition

Instructions: First read it independently, then tear along the line to make a new poem.

|

|

The silence stretches, vast and wide,
But in its depths, a voice survived.
The boards splinter beneath my feet,
Yet through the cracks, the light breaks free.
The tide was never mine to tame,
It only mirrored borrowed shame.
The wounds still burn, the scars still ache,
But healing rises in their wake.
The ruin wasn't meant to end me.
The echoes fade, they hold no weight.
I see them now—too little, too late.
A throne of gold, now set aflame,
And yet, the fire does not take my name.
I step into the blaze, unafraid.

|

|

STAGE 2

Ashen Veil

The Weight of an Open Sky

It's Gone!
The burden, the stage–
Vanished in plain sight
Who knew it would take
Just the flicker of a light?

It's Done!
Those terrors, those cries–
Destroyed through faith
Who knew it would take
Just a choice I dared to make?

And yet..

My feet shift uncomfortably,
Unaware how to dance now
How to jump and reach these open skies
That I have died for

The wind suddenly howling through empty space,
a hollow symphony of beginnings.
The thrill, the tremor—
Is this **freedom** or **fear**?

It's almost as if
My hands reach out on their own
To grasp onto a new blueprint and redesign
To move, to scream? speak, to build

Find an anchor, a guide,
Even a sign will do
For this uncertainty seems unnerving
And thrilling, all at once
But alas- there is nothing
The mirage screen has lifted
And all that stands is the wide open sky,
My trembling pulse,
My pockets full of knowledge
A golden path - where new dreams lie!

Echoes in the Ashes

I take that first step
Unfurl my hands,
Stare at the pathway

Feeling the warm and
Cold ground beneath me
I swing in that feeling

Then I turn, more like swirl
Trip over upon seeing
The ashes beside me

The ghosts of my pasts
That I happily laid down to rest
Will they haunt me?
Well, I'll avoid them to my best

Looking forward I see the blues
Golden shimmer and orange dews
The sky changing as if I've canvassed it myself

I plan my days ahead,
Take it a step a day.
Breathe every time I see the ashes

Never once looking at my gold caches.

The Cycle of Rebuilding

Days pass to no end,
I grow tired of this newfound freedom
Finally risking a peek at the ruins behind me—
The ashes still present, mixed in the floor below,
Gold splattered like wounds that won't close.

Of course—let's rebuild!
For I am a masterpiece after all,
Every masterpiece requires a stage frame
And this time, the frame's mine to design.

The world tilts its head, curious, watching.
"What are you building?" it asks.
"A monument, a masterpiece," I reply,
Hands stained with molten purpose.

I try again.
Build again.
Fail again.
But try again.

I grasp again that horrifying gold,
Hold onto the demons of the old,
Desperately despising the ruins

While eager to rebuild the illusion.

The echoes murmur, hum through the air,
"Did you not burn this before?"
And I falter, my hands still crafting.
Of course I did. *Of course I did.*

"You know how this ends," I whisper to myself.
And yet, I sculpt, I forge, I mold, I weave.
New visions, new lines, yet the same old seams.
The blueprints change, but the shape remains,
A gilded silhouette of ghosts.

This is baffling, and I'm going crazy,
Looping through echoes that will not forsake me.
"Is this all I know?"
The thought carves itself into the walls,
Etching doubts between the layers.

"But is it yours?" the world asks again.
Am I the architect, or merely a vessel,
Redesigning ruins I cannot escape?

For the first time, I pause.
I look at my gold-stained hands—trembling.
And I do not build.

The Ending Before the Beginning

I stood at the edge of the world,
Afraid to step forward,
Afraid to step back,
Suspended in the in-between.
Memories like anchors,
Fears like ghosts,
Every possibility a trembling thread.
And then I fell—
Into the unknown, into the fire, into myself.
Only to wake up,
Back at the edge of the world.

Burning Questions

The now everburning fire asks me, about myself
Talking to me like we are one,
These "What if" questions flow through
And I must tell you, they enlighten me
You must try them too!

The hours on the clock tick by,
As I spend every second beckoning
No longer questioning
An urge to physically push through these bonds–
Bonds that my fire has already burned,
yet somehow they still exist - I see them.

In my mind? In my soul? In my home? – I can't tell.
They're blurred through my opaque lenses
An illusion once again? Maybe,
But they signify something,

An unbroken promise, a faith, a shackled life

"What If?"

What if you had chosen differently?
What if you had spoken when you stayed silent,
or walked away when you held on?
What if you had broken the rules before they broke you?
Would you be freer, wilder—more alive?
Or would you still be chasing, still rewriting,
still waiting for a moment that never comes?
What if the past wasn't set in stone?
What if regret was just a shadow,
cast by the light of everything you still could be?
Would you rewrite it? Would you dare?
Or would you find that, even now,
you are exactly where you were meant to stand?
And what if... just this once...
I stop asking?
What if I just **live**?

A Masterpiece Without a Frame

All my life, I have done and erased
Chasing echoes, caught in a haze.
I've burned, I've woven, shaped with fire,
Yet golden cages rose ever higher.
I called them stages, called them fate
A masterpiece, but only with a frame
Was I ever the artist at all,
Or just a player bound to the call

But what if the stage was never real,
A story sold, a tethered ideal?
What if the world was never a cage,
And I was free before the stage?
What if the stage does not need to be
And I can just be a masterpiece of complexity
Instead, the **world** becomes my platform
And I'm no longer its gilded pawn

The Midas touch fades into dust,
No longer weighed by shine or rust.
I walk unbound, not seeking more,
For worth was always in the core - never in the lore.
Not in the building, not in the fall,

Not in the hands that shape it all.
The world is vast, and so am I,
Not framed, not staged—just alive.

The Unmaking of the Stage

The stage in my mind collapsed a while ago,
But my hands were still aboard
Moulding and reshaping, wailing and venting

The stage, I have now let go of,
Seeking freedom -
Freedom to choose - choose whether I want a stage or a
guitar
Freedom to express - express all of my deepest desires
Freedom to lose - lose my mind and drive insanity
Freedom to be Free - free of my inner gilded canopy

And this freedom I speak of
No longer requires destruction,
It's more brutal for it desires creation
Creation through knowledge - and I NEED TO KNOW.

The Clearing

Facing the mirror, I see my rain-soaked face—
The horrors that bled through my tears
Now stain my cheeks and speak louder than any words.

The battle that has run through my mind
Is finally ending,
The storm cloud bursting,
Leaving white skies above.

Clearer than ever, I see myself in plain sight:
A mind once frail, once shriveled
From the all-consuming sewage water,
Now exposed to fresh air for the first time.

The battle has left its marks (sure)
In wounded synapses and bled-through thought,
But beneath these scars lies something unexpected—
A foundation not of gold or ash or stage,
But of bedrock I never knew existed.

I trace the patterns of rain on my face,
Feel where the tears have carved new channels,
And realize—this weathering was not destruction,
But the necessary erosion of what was false.

The mirror no longer shows what others built,
But what remains when it all washes away.
Not an ending, not quite a beginning,
But the sacred pause between breaths
Where possibility waits, unadorned.

My hands, clean of gold dust at last,
Reach toward the clearing sky.

Stage 3

Unbound Flame

The Library of Self

I walk through the endless stacks,
Each spine a different possibility.
Shakespeare's sonnets—teaching me
That love persists beyond reason and time.

The Financial Times—revealing
How empires rise and fall on human psychology,
More than numbers and graphs.

Plato's Republic—showing how
We've questioned the same truths
Since we first gazed at shadows on cave walls.

A heavy tome on quantum physics falls open—
Teaching me that observation creates reality,
That nothing is fixed until witnessed.

I pass my fingers over Mary Wollstonecraft,
Who knew two centuries ago
What many still struggle to accept:
That freedom cannot be partial.

I pull Maya Angelou from the shelf,
Her words singing of cages and wings,

Of rising despite history's weight.

Between Hafiz and Rumi,
I find mystic truth:
That the divine and human
Were never truly separate.

Today I read Marcus Aurelius,
Tomorrow perhaps bell hooks,
The day after, maybe Lao Tzu.

Each book another room in myself
I never knew existed.
Each page a mirror reflecting
Not who I am,
But who I might become.

The greatest revelation:
I am both reader and writer,
Both the empty page
And the ink that fills it.

Awakening

I CAN SEE NOW,
Everything that everyone hid me from hid from me,

The over-pouring love, full of light
That is now guiding me
Comes from within (finally!)

The guide to my life - visible now
An unwritten book, never held by anyone
Mine to write, to tear apart,
to rewrite as many times as I need.
I'm ALIVE and life is mine to take,

The scaffolding falls away to reveal
Not perfection, but presence.
Not answers, but space for questions.
Not a destination, but a path that shifts with each step.
This is the map I follow now.

Not to conquer or control,
But to inhabit with presence.
To walk with eyes that see clearly
The difference between what was given
And what I've chosen to carry.

My silence is no longer emptiness
But the sacred pause between breaths
Where wisdom gathers and waits
For actions born of clarity,
Not reaction, not performance.

The mirror shows me unadorned—
Both wounded and whole,
Both student and teacher,
Both the work and the artist.
And in this seeing, I begin.

Cartography of Liberation

Find your place on this living map.
Your breath marks the starting point.
All great changes begin right here.

Gandhi walked paths of peaceful salt.
Parks sat firmly on divided lines.
Truth spoke loudly against chains.

Liberty moves through hardship.
The route demands your courage.
No true freedom comes with ease.

Tubman returned nineteen times.
She risked all to guide others.
Freedom's work is always shared.

Mandela emerged from twenty-seven years imprisoned
With forgiveness, not vengeance.
The map says: Walls become doors with time.

Study the Haitian Revolution,
The first successful slave uprising,
How the impossible becomes inevitable
When justice finds its moment.

Stonewall's rebels stood firm.
Suffragettes refused to eat.
Warsaw fighters faced tanks.
Not by victories alone,
but by the audacity of attempt.

Now draw your own route.
Begin where you stand.
Use their stars for navigation,
But trust your own compass.

The truest map reveals itself in motion.
Each step forward alters the landscape.
Liberation is not a destination
But the courage to journey unmapped.

Freedom lives in movement.

The Dialogue of Questions

What if knowledge is not the filling of a vessel,
But the kindling of a flame?

> — Socrates never actually said this,
> but lived it through endless questions.

What if uncertainty is not weakness,
But the beginning of wisdom?

> — Montaigne understood this,
> writing "Que sais-je?" (What do I know?)
> above his study door.

What if your wounds are not flaws,
But openings to greater understanding?

> — Kintsugi masters repair broken pottery
> with gold, making fractures the most precious part.

What if power is not control over others,
But mastery of yourself?

> — Marcus Aurelius ruled an empire
> but wrote: "You have power over your mind,
> not outside events."

What if success is not acquisition,
But contribution?

— Jonas Salk refused to patent his polio vaccine,
saying: "Could you patent the sun?"

What if wealth is not what you have,
But what you can live without?
— Diogenes lived in a barrel,
yet Alexander the Great said,
"Were I not Alexander, I would be Diogenes."

What if transformation is not instantaneous,
But daily practice?
— The Buddha taught:
"Drop by drop is the water pot filled."

What if you are not one self,
But many possibilities?
— Walt Whitman wrote:
"I contain multitudes."

What if the questions themselves
Are more valuable than any answers?

Unscripted

Them: You've changed.

                    Me: Yes, I finally recognized myself.

Them: You used to be more...

                            Me: More what?

Them: Accommodating. Predictable.

               Me: I accommodated everyone but myself.

Them: That's harsh.

                        Me: That's honest.

Them: We miss the old you.

                  Me: Freedom begins with truth.

Them: What happened?

               Me: I stopped waiting for permission.

Them: To do what?

                  Me: To exist on my own terms.

Them: That sounds selfish.

      Me: It would have been selfish to keep pretending.

Them: We're just concerned.

              Me: About me, or about your comfort?

Them: Both, I suppose.

                Me: Growth requires discomfort.

Them: Will you come back?

                           Me: To what?

Them: To us. To how things were.

Me: No. But I'm here now, more fully than before.

Them: I don't understand.

Me: You don't have to understand to respect it.

Them: Then how do we move forward?

Me: By meeting each other where we are,

Not where we wish the other would be.

Them: That's... difficult.

Me: Life happens in the difficult spaces.

Them: What do you need from me?

Me: To be seen, not fixed.

Them: And what can I expect from you?

Me: Authenticity. Not perfection.

Them: I can try that.

Me: That's all I'm asking.

Them: Is this goodbye, then?

Me: No. It's hello.

For the first time.

Them: I'm listening.

Me: Then we've already begun

The truth is hidden in plain sight—read only the last line
of my responses to uncover it.

A Conversation Across Time

I met my younger self for coffee,
In a quiet corner of an old café,
The kind that smells of nostalgia
And whispers of stories long past.

She sat there, wide-eyed, restless fingers tapping,
A cup untouched, steam swirling between us like fate.
She looked at me like a puzzle,
Trying to solve what she would someday become.

"So?" she asked. "Did we make it?"

I smiled, stirring my drink,
Watching the past and present ripple together.
"We did. But not in the way you think."

She frowned. "Did we win? Did we prove them wrong?"

I sighed, the weight of her questions
Like echoes of old battles I no longer fight.
"There was nothing to prove, little one.
No enemy to conquer but ourselves."

She scoffed. "That sounds like something an old person
would say."

I laughed, because I once would've said the same.

"Remember the fire? The stage? The ruins?"
She nods, eyes darkening.
"I burned it all," she says proudly.
"And then rebuilt it," I remind her.

Her hands tighten around her cup.
"I had to."

I nod, leaning closer.
"But did you ever ask yourself—why?"

She freezes.
And I see it—the realization dawning.
The endless cycles, the rebuilding of cages,
The belief that freedom meant destruction,
That worth meant proving,
That existence meant struggle.

For the first time, she looks tired.

"What if I don't build again?" she whispers.
"What if I just... be?"

I reach across the table, fingers brushing hers,
A connection across time, across growth,
Across all the battles we thought defined us.
"Then," I say, "you will finally be free."

She lets out a breath, one she's held for years.
And then, for the first time,
She picks up her coffee—
And drinks.

Helix of Becoming

I shed the skin of yesterday's self. A snake doesn't mourn its old scales.
The caterpillar dissolves completely Before butterfly wings can form.
Ancient Egyptians called this "kheper" Transformation through sacred scarab.

I translate the hieroglyphs of my past, Finding meaning in ancient wounds.
Thich Nhat Hanh teaches: "No mud,   No lotus." Beauty requires depth.
The olive's bitter fruit yields   The sweetest oil when pressed.

I study the renaissance masters who   Created masterpieces through constraint.
Da Vinci filled notebooks with questions Before he filled canvases with answers.
Einstein imagined riding light beams   Before writing theories of relativity.

I balance action with reflection,   Like breathing in and breathing out.
Wu wei—the Taoist "non-action"—   Is effort aligned

with natural flow.
The oak grows rings in silence   While standing fully in
each storm.

I embrace both shadow and illumination, As Jung taught
about wholeness.
Dickinson found universe in solitude,   Baldwin found it
in confrontation.
Different paths to the same summit,   As the Buddha
described reality.

I weave together disparate threads: Science, art,
philosophy, faith.
Leonardo knew anatomy and painting,   Hypatia knew
stars and mathematics.
Da Gama navigated by both stars   And the wisdom of
local guides.

I learn that growth isn't linear   But spiraling through
familiar points.
Each rotation brings deeper knowing—   What was once
concept becomes embodied.
The ancients carved spirals on stones   Marking cosmic
cycles of return.

Midas Unlearned

For years I thought my curse was touching things
that turned to gold but withered in my hands.
The curse was thinking gold was what I wanted.

History whispers this lesson repeatedly:
King Midas starved surrounded by wealth.
Croesus fell despite his riches.
Empires collapsed under golden weight.

I studied their mistakes like sacred texts,
Searching for the incantation to reverse the spell.
But the answer wasn't in amassing more
or turning away from abundance entirely.

The alchemist's true secret:
Transmutation works both ways.
Gold back to bread. Statues back to loved ones.
Possession back to appreciation.

The trick wasn't in my hands but in my seeing.
Touch the world not to own it,
but to feel its texture,
its heat, its pulse beneath your fingers.

I learned to ask: What nourishes?
What sustains beyond the moment?
What grows when shared rather than hoarded?

Now I touch leaves and feel their veins,
Hold water and marvel at its clarity,
Grasp dirt and sense the universe it contains.
None of it mine. All of it gift.

The curse lifted when I stopped
calling it a blessing.

I am

I am whole.
Not despite my breaks,
But because of how I've mended.
The gold that fills my cracks is mine now—
Not gilded cage but chosen adornment, hard-earned
light.
I walk the world differently now, feet touching earth
with intention.
The structures I build serve only to shelter, never to
contain what cannot be contained.
I remember who I was before the stage was built. Before
applause became both currency and chains.
I've counted backwards to zero, found the child who
knew how to play without performing, how to be
without proving.
Time moves differently in this space—circular, not linear.
Each moment both beginning and completion.
The voice in my head speaks in my own language now. I
recognize its cadence, its truth.
I have learned that solitude is not loneliness but
necessary communion.
I have learned that presence requires no announcement.
I have learned that my worth was never in question.
Only my willingness to claim it.

Only my courage to live it.
Only my choice.
And I choose.
I am.

The Last Word

You have walked through these pages,
Stumbled over the same questions,
Felt the weight of every almost,
Listened to voices—yours, theirs, and the ones that never
spoke.
And now, you are here.
Not at the end,
But at the beginning.
(*The last word is yours.*)